FOR THE RECORD

A PERSONAL FACTS & DOCUMENT ORGANIZER

BY RICKI PAGANO

FIVE STAR **PUBLICATIONS**
INCORPORATED
Chandler, AZ USA

Linda F. Radke, President
Five Star Publications, Inc.
PO Box 6698
Chandler, AZ 85246-6698
480-940-8182 Fax: 480-940-8787

www.ForTheRecordBook.com
www.FiveStarPublications.com

Library of Congress Cataloging-in-Publication Data

Pagano, Ricki.
 For the record : a personal facts & document organizer / by Ricki Pagano.
-- 3rd ed.
      p. cm.
 "A comprehensive series of forms where you can record and keep track of
virtually every bit of personal information"--P.   .
 ISBN-13: 978-1-58985-058-3
 ISBN-10: 1-58985-058-0
 1. Family records--Forms. 2. Finance, Personal--Forms. 3. Estate
planning--Forms. 4. Family records--Management. 5. Legal
documents--Management. I. Title.
 HF5736.P295 2007
 640--dc22
                                2006038361

Third Edition

Printed in the United States of America

Editor: Salvatore Caputo
Cover Design: Kris Taft Miller
Interior Layout and Design: Janet Bergin

A Message from Ricki Sue Pagano

As a social worker (MSW, CISW) in the field of geriatric care management, I saw firsthand how important it is for people to have a sense of control over their lives. This sense of control calms them when life all around them is stormy, and it gives them the confidence to enjoy the good times as well.

How do we gain a sense of control, though?

I believe preparation and organization are the keys, and that *For the Record* will help you be prepared for any event or need by giving you a single place to organize the details of your life.

For the Record is a comprehensive series of forms where you can record and keep track of virtually every bit of personal information: Social Security numbers and birthdays, insurance policies and prescriptions, even what you want your family to do when you die.

I realize that a series of forms can't cover your every need, so I've also included note pages where you can customize your *For the Record* to your unique needs. For instance, one woman told me she would write down the names of all the individuals to be contacted when she died on the extra pages included in the Final Arrangements section. Another gentleman actually wrote his own funeral service and put it in there.

Truly, the uses of *For the Record* are endless.

In the Family Information section, you might add family memories or a family tree.

In the Medical section, you could note any special treatments or where you obtained such items as glasses, dentures or hearing aids. This is also a place where you can write down your instructions for emergencies, who to call and what to do, even instructions for taking care of a pet while you're unavailable. You could also note your preferences for a home health agency or assisted living or a skilled nursing facility.

Use the Insurance section as a place to keep detailed descriptions of your coverage, to track insurance payments and claims filed.

The employment section is a good place to write down the names, addresses, and phone numbers of your references.

In the Income/Expenses section, you may want to record all of your newspaper and magazine subscriptions and track their renewal dates.

The Legal section is a good place to record the location of your documents (legal, education records, business, etc.)

The Personal Property Inventory is also a place to include background information, memories and photos of family heirlooms. It's also a good place to keep track of home improvements and to itemize household furnishings, electronics and appliances. Make note, too, of where you keep the manuals and warranty information.

Perhaps you never thought of the various repair services you use as Important Phone Numbers, but when an appliance or your home-security system goes on the fritz, you'll be thankful you recorded them here.

I hope that *For the Record* will provide you with the opportunity to organize the details of your life. If you take the time to fill out every page, you'll have a handy reference book that will allow you and your loved ones to find important information easily and quickly. That should take some of the stress out of emergencies. May it also give you the comfort of knowing that you've taken charge of all of life's details.

TABLE OF CONTENTS

PERSONAL & FAMILY INFORMATION   1

MEDICAL   10

INSURANCE   15

LEGAL INFORMATION/ DOCUMENT LOCATOR   20

EMPLOYMENT   23

INCOME / EXPENSES   26

FINANCIAL ASSETS / LIABILITIES   30

RETIREMENT ACCOUNTS   42

FINAL ARRANGEMENTS   45

IMPORTANT TELEPHONE NUMBERS   48

PERSONAL PROPERTY INVENTORY   54

APPENDIX   65

PERSONAL
& FAMILY
INFORMATION

PERSONAL & FAMILY INFORMATION

Name

Address

Phone _____ Mobile

Fax _____ E-mail

Business Address

Phone _____ Mobile _____ Fax/E-mail

Date of Birth

Place of Birth

Social Security #

Marital Status

Citizenship

Military

Passport #

Driver's License #

In Case of Emergency Please Notify:

Name

Address

Phone _____ Mobile

Fax _____ E-mail

Family Information

Name of Spouse
_____

    Address
_____

    Phone _____ Mobile _____

    Fax _____ E-mail _____

    Business Address
_____

    Phone _____ Mobile _____ Fax/E-mail _____

Date of Birth
_____

Place of Birth
_____

Social Security #
_____

Marital Status
_____

Citizenship
_____

Military
_____

Passport #
_____

Driver's License #
_____

Spouse's Mother
_____

    Address
_____

    Phone _____ Mobile _____ Fax/E-mail _____

Spouse's Father
_____

    Address
_____

    Phone _____ Mobile _____ Fax/E-mail _____

Family Information

Name of Mother
_____

    Address
_____

    Phone _____ Mobile _____ Fax/E-mail _____

Name of Father
_____

    Address
_____

    Phone _____ Mobile _____ Fax/E-mail _____

Sibling #1 Name
_____

    Address
_____

    Phone _____ Mobile _____ Fax/E-mail _____

Sibling #2 Name
_____

    Address
_____

    Phone _____ Mobile _____ Fax/E-mail _____

Sibling #3 Name
_____

    Address
_____

    Phone _____ Mobile _____ Fax/E-mail _____

Sibling #4 Name
_____

    Address
_____

    Phone _____ Mobile _____ Fax/E-mail _____

FAMILY INFORMATION

Child #1 Name

Address

Phone   Mobile   Fax/E-mail

Date of Birth

Place of Birth

Social Security #

Child #2 Name

Address

Phone   Mobile   Fax/E-mail

Date of Birth

Place of Birth

Social Security #

Child #3 Name

Address

Phone   Mobile   Fax/E-mail

Date of Birth

Place of Birth

Social Security #

FAMILY INFORMATION

Child #4 Name

Address

Phone	Mobile	Fax/E-mail

Date of Birth

Place of Birth

Social Security #

Child #5 Name

Address

Phone	Mobile	Fax/E-mail

Date of Birth

Place of Birth

Social Security #

Child #6 Name

Address

Phone	Mobile	Fax/E-mail

Date of Birth

Place of Birth

Social Security #

FAMILY INFORMATION

Significant Other

    Relationship

    Address

    Phone   Mobile   Fax/E-mail

Significant Other

    Relationship

    Address

    Phone   Mobile   Fax/E-mail

Significant Other

    Relationship

    Address

    Phone   Mobile   Fax/E-mail

Significant Other

    Relationship

    Address

    Phone   Mobile   Fax/E-mail

PROFESSIONAL/SOCIAL MEMBERSHIPS

Organization name

Address

Phone   Mobile   Fax/E-mail

ID #

Organization name

Address

Phone   Mobile   Fax/E-mail

ID #

Organization name

Address

Phone   Mobile   Fax/E-mail

ID #

Organization name

Address

Phone   Mobile   Fax/E-mail

ID #

NOTES

MEDICAL

MEDICAL INFORMATION

Physician's Name

    Specialization

    Address

    Phone   Mobile   Fax/E-mail

Physician's Name

    Specialization

    Address

    Phone   Mobile   Fax/E-mail

Physician's Name

    Specialization

    Address

    Phone   Mobile   Fax/E-mail

Physician's Name

    Specialization

    Address

    Phone   Mobile   Fax/E-mail

Medical Information

Physician's Name

    Specialization

    Address

    Phone   Mobile   Fax/E-mail

Physician's Name

    Specialization

    Address

    Phone   Mobile   Fax/E-mail

Physician's Name

    Specialization

    Address

    Phone   Mobile   Fax/E-mail

Physician's Name

    Specialization

    Address

    Phone   Mobile   Fax/E-mail

MEDICAL INFORMATION

Medical/Surgical History – Date of Onset/Diagnosis

1. _____
2. _____
3. _____
4. _____
5. _____
6. _____
7. _____
8. _____
9. _____
10. _____

Medications/Treatments – Name/Dosage/Diagnosis

1. _____
2. _____
3. _____
4. _____
5. _____
6. _____
7. _____
8. _____
9. _____
10. _____

Allergies _____

Hospital/Ambulance Membership _____

Code Status _____

Dietary Restrictions _____

MEDICAL INFORMATION

Family History _____

_____

Pharmacy _____

Address _____

Phone _____ Mobile _____ Fax/E-mail _____

Long Term Care Preference _____

_____

NOTES

_____

_____

_____

_____

_____

_____

_____

_____

_____

_____

_____

INSURANCE

INSURANCE INFORMATION

Primary Medical Insurance
_____

Agent/Broker
_____

Address
_____

Phone   Mobile   Fax/E-mail
_____

Policy #
_____

Supplemental Medical Insurance
_____

Agent/Broker
_____

Address
_____

Phone   Mobile   Fax/E-mail
_____

Policy #
_____

Home Health or Long Term Care Policy
_____

Agent/Broker
_____

Address
_____

Phone   Mobile   Fax/E-mail
_____

Policy #
_____

Life Insurance
_____

Agent/Broker
_____

Address
_____

Phone   Mobile   Fax/E-mail
_____

Policy #
_____

INSURANCE INFORMATION

Disability Income Insurance

Agent/Broker

Address

Phone   Mobile   Fax/E-mail

Policy #

Accidental Death Insurance

Agent/Broker

Address

Phone   Mobile   Fax/E-mail

Policy #

Homeowner's Insurance

Agent/Broker

Address

Phone   Mobile   Fax/E-mail

Policy #

Auto Insurance

Agent/Broker

Address

Phone   Mobile   Fax/E-mail

Policy #

INSURANCE INFORMATION

Mortgage Insurance

Agent/Broker

Address

Phone   Mobile   Fax/E-mail

Policy #

Credit Card Insurance

Agent/Broker

Address

Phone   Mobile   Fax/E-mail

Policy #

Other Insurance

Agent/Broker

Address

Phone   Mobile   Fax/E-mail

Policy #

Other Insurance

Agent/Broker

Address

Phone   Mobile   Fax/E-mail

Policy #

NOTES

LEGAL INFORMATION/ DOCUMENT LOCATOR

LEGAL INFORMATION/DOCUMENT LOCATOR

Attorney's Name

Address

Phone   Mobile

Fax   E-mail

Location of Legal Documents

Will

Trust

Medical Power of Attorney

Financial Power of Attorney

Living Will/Pre-hospital Directive

Guardian/Conservator

Location of Personal Documents

Birth Certificates

Marriage License

Divorce Decree

Adoption and Custody Papers

Citizenship Papers

Social Security Cards

Passports/Visas

Voter Registration

Spare house and car keys

Legal Information/Document Locator

Insurance Policies

Employment Records/Corporate Records

Education Records/Diplomas

Financial Statement

Loan Documents

Real Estate Documents

Investment Documents/Certificates

Bank Statements/Cancelled Checks

Tax Returns

Motor Vehicle Titles

Notes

EMPLOYMENT

EMPLOYMENT HISTORY

Present Employer

Address

Phone   Mobile   Fax/E-mail

Position Title

Date of Hire

Salary

Benefits

1.

2.

3.

4.

5.

Previous Employer

Address

Phone   Mobile   Fax/E-mail

Date of Employment

Salary

Previous Employer

Address

Phone   Mobile   Fax/E-mail

Date of Employment

Salary

Notes

INCOME / EXPENSES

INCOME

Monthly Income	Yourself	Spouse
Salary and entitlements	_____	_____
Commissions	_____	_____
Dividends	_____	_____
Interest	_____	_____
Rentals	_____	_____
Alimony	_____	_____
Child Support	_____	_____
Maintenance	_____	_____
Other	_____	_____

Annual Income	Yourself	Spouse
	_____	_____

MONTHLY EXPENSES

	Average Amount	Time of Month Due
Mortgage/Rent #1 Home	_____	_____
Other Real Estate	_____	_____
Electric	_____	_____
Gas	_____	_____
Water	_____	_____
Garbage	_____	_____
Phone	_____	_____
Cable	_____	_____
Food	_____	_____
Medication	_____	_____
Medical Equipment and Rental/supplies	_____	_____
Credit Cards	Average Amount	Time of Month Due
1. _____	_____	_____
2. _____	_____	_____
3. _____	_____	_____
4. _____	_____	_____
5. _____	_____	_____
6. _____	_____	_____
Insurance		
1. _____	_____	_____
2. _____	_____	_____
3. _____	_____	_____
4. _____	_____	_____
5. _____	_____	_____
6. _____	_____	_____

MONTHLY EXPENSES

Loans Payable to Banks and Installment Contracts Payable

1. _____

2. _____

3. _____

4. _____

Other	Average Amount	Time of Month Due
1. _____	_____	_____
2. _____	_____	_____
3. _____	_____	_____

Location of Unpaid Bills _____

_____

_____

NOTES

_____

_____

_____

_____

_____

_____

_____

FINANCIAL ASSETS/ LIABILITIES

ASSETS

Cash in bank:

Checking Account

Savings

CDs

IRA

Other retirement accounts

Due from friends/relatives

Mortgage and Contracts for Deed owned

Securities

Cash Surrender Value Life Insurance

Home

Other Real Estate

Automobiles

Personal Property

Other Assets

1.

2.

3.

4.

5.

LIABILITIES

Loans payable to banks

Loans payable to others

Installment contracts payable

Amounts due to retail stores

Credit cards

Income taxes payable

Other taxes payable

Loans of life insurance

Mortgage on home

Mortgage or liens on other real estate owned

Contracts for deed

Other Liabilities

Total Liabilities:

FINANCIAL INFORMATION

Bank Name
_____

    Address
_____

    Phone   Fax
_____

Checking account #
_____

Savings account #
_____

Money market account #
_____

CDs account #
_____

Safety deposit box #   Key location
_____

    Contents
_____

_____

Bank Name
_____

    Address
_____

    Phone   Fax
_____

Checking account #
_____

Savings account #
_____

Money market account #
_____

CDs account #
_____

Safety deposit box #   Key location
_____

    Contents
_____

_____

_____

Financial Information

Bank Name

    Address

    Phone   Fax

Checking account #

Savings account #

Money market account #

CDs account #

Safety deposit box #   Key location

    Contents

Bank Name

    Address

    Phone   Fax

Checking account #

Savings account #

Money market account #

CDs account #

Safety deposit box #   Key location

    Contents

FINANCIAL INFORMATION

Bank Name

Address

Phone   Fax

Checking account #

Savings account #

Money market account #

CDs account #

Safety deposit box #   Key location

Contents

Bank Name

Address

Phone   Fax

Checking account #

Savings account #

Money market account #

CDs account #

Safety deposit box #   Key location

Contents

FINANCIAL INFORMATION

A. Due from Friends/Relatives

	Name of Debtor	Owed to	Collateral	How Payable	Date Due
1.					
2.					
3.					

B. Mortgages and contracts for deed owned

	Name of Debtor	Owed to	Collateral	How Payable	Date Due
1.					
2.					
3.					

C. Life Insurance

	Insured	Ins. Co.	Beneficiary	Face Value	Cash Value	Loans
1.						
2.						
3.						

D. Securities Owned

	# Shares	Description	Name Registered	Cost
1.				
2.				
3.				

FINANCIAL INFORMATION

Securities owned

5. _____

6. _____

7. _____

8. _____

9. _____

10. _____

11. _____

12. _____

13. _____

14. _____

E. Real Estate

Address & type of property	Title names	Mo. income	Cost	yr. Acquired	Ins. amt
1.					
2.					
3.					

F. Mortgages or liens on real estate

To whom payable	How payable	Interest Rate	Maturity date
1.			
2.			
3.			
4.			

Financial Information

G. Loans payable to banks and installment contracts payable

To whom payable	Address	Collateral	How payable	Maturity date
1.				
2.				
3.				
4.				

H. Other

1. _____
2. _____
3. _____
4. _____
5. _____

CREDIT CARD INFORMATION

Company name

Address

Phone   Fax   E-mail

Card #

Expiration Date

Company name

Address

Phone   Fax   E-mail

Card #

Expiration Date

Company name

Address

Phone   Fax   E-mail

Card #

Expiration Date

Company name

Address

Phone   Fax   E-mail

Card #

Expiration Date

CREDIT CARD INFORMATION

Company name

Address

Phone   Fax   E-mail

Card #

Expiration Date

Company name

Address

Phone   Fax   E-mail

Card #

Expiration Date

Company name

Address

Phone   Fax   E-mail

Card #

Expiration Date

Company name

Address

Phone   Fax   E-mail

Card #

Expiration Date

NOTES

RETIREMENT ACCOUNTS

RETIREMENT ACCOUNTS

401K/IRAs

Investment description

1. _____

2. _____

3. _____

4. _____

Other Funds

Investment description

1. _____

2. _____

3. _____

4. _____

5. _____

6. _____

7. _____

8. _____

9. _____

10. _____

11. _____

12. _____

13. _____

14. _____

Retirement Accounts

15. _____

16. _____

17. _____

18. _____

19. _____

20. _____

Notes

_____

_____

_____

_____

_____

_____

_____

_____

_____

_____

_____

_____

FINAL ARRANGEMENTS

Final Arrangements

Mortuary Name _____

    Address _____

    Phone _____ Fax _____

    E-mail _____

    Contact person _____

Cemetery Name _____

    Address _____

    Phone _____ Fax _____

    E-mail _____

    Contact person _____

Church, Synagogue or Place of Worship _____

    Address _____

    Phone _____ Fax _____

    E-mail _____

    Contact person _____

Organ Donor _____

Casket _____

Burial instructions _____

_____

FINAL ARRANGEMENTS

Special instructions for service

_____

_____

_____

_____

NOTES

_____

_____

_____

_____

_____

_____

_____

_____

_____

_____

_____

_____

IMPORTANT TELEPHONE NUMBERS

IMPORTANT NUMBERS

Accountant
_____

    Address
_____

    Phone   Mobile   Fax/E-mail
_____

Auto Repair
_____

    Address
_____

    Phone   Mobile   Fax/E-mail
_____

Carpet Cleaning
_____

    Address
_____

    Phone   Mobile   Fax/E-mail
_____

Caterer
_____

    Address
_____

    Phone   Mobile   Fax/E-mail
_____

Child Care
_____

    Address
_____

    Phone   Mobile   Fax/E-mail
_____

Church, Synagogue or Place of Worship
_____

    Address
_____

    Phone   Mobile   Fax/E-mail
_____

Cleaners
_____

    Address
_____

    Phone   Mobile   Fax/E-mail
_____

Important Numbers

Computer Repair

    Address

    Phone   Mobile   Fax/E-mail

Electrician

    Address

    Phone   Mobile   Fax/E-mail

Exterminator

    Address

    Phone   Mobile   Fax/E-mail

Financial Planner

    Address

    Phone   Mobile   Fax/E-mail

Florist

    Address

    Phone   Mobile   Fax/E-mail

Hairdresser

    Address

    Phone   Mobile   Fax/E-mail

Health Club

    Address

    Phone   Mobile   Fax/E-mail

Important Numbers

Housecleaning
_____

    Address
_____

    Phone   Mobile   Fax/E-mail

Landscaping
_____

    Address
_____

    Phone   Mobile   Fax/E-mail

Moving Service
_____

    Address
_____

    Phone   Mobile   Fax/E-mail

Pharmacy
_____

    Address
_____

    Phone   Mobile   Fax/E-mail

Plumber
_____

    Address
_____

    Phone   Mobile   Fax/E-mail

Pool Service
_____

    Address
_____

    Phone   Mobile   Fax/E-mail

Propane Service
_____

    Address
_____

    Phone   Mobile   Fax/E-mail

Important Numbers

Realtor _____

   Address _____

   Phone _____ Mobile _____ Fax/E-mail _____

Security System _____

   Address _____

   Phone _____ Mobile _____ Fax/E-mail _____

Solar Heating Repair _____

   Address _____

   Phone _____ Mobile _____ Fax/E-mail _____

Sprinkler Repair _____

   Address _____

   Phone _____ Mobile _____ Fax/E-mail _____

Transportation _____

   Address _____

   Phone _____ Mobile _____ Fax/E-mail _____

Travel Agent _____

   Address _____

   Phone _____ Mobile _____ Fax/E-mail _____

Veterinary Care _____

   Address _____

   Phone _____ Mobile _____ Fax/E-mail _____

NOTES

PERSONAL PROPERTY INVENTORY

PERSONAL PROPERTY INVENTORY

Item   Value

Jewelry

1. _____   _____

2. _____   _____

3. _____   _____

4. _____   _____

5. _____   _____

6. _____   _____

7. _____   _____

8. _____   _____

9. _____   _____

10. _____   _____

Art

1. _____   _____

2. _____   _____

3. _____   _____

4. _____   _____

5. _____   _____

6. _____   _____

7. _____   _____

8. _____   _____

	Item	Value

Collectibles

1. _____   _____

2. _____   _____

3. _____   _____

4. _____   _____

5. _____   _____

6. _____   _____

7. _____   _____

8. _____   _____

Clothing

1. _____   _____

2. _____   _____

3. _____   _____

4. _____   _____

5. _____   _____

6. _____   _____

7. _____   _____

8. _____   _____

Furnishings

1. _____   _____

2. _____   _____

Item	Value

Furnishings Cont.

3. _____   _____

4. _____   _____

5. _____   _____

6. _____   _____

7. _____   _____

8. _____   _____

9. _____   _____

10._____   _____

11._____   _____

12._____   _____

Other

1. _____   _____

2. _____   _____

3. _____   _____

4. _____   _____

5. _____   _____

6. _____   _____

7. _____   _____

8. _____   _____

9. _____   _____

10._____   _____

Item	Value
Other Cont.	
11._____	_____
12._____	_____
13._____	_____
14._____	_____
15._____	_____
16._____	_____
17._____	_____
18._____	_____
19._____	_____
20._____	_____

NOTES

_____

_____

_____

_____

_____

_____

_____

_____

_____

_____

NOTES

NOTES

NOTES

NOTES

NOTES

NOTES

APPENDIX

APPENDIX

Tax Records to Keep

Records of Income Received

Expense Items — work related ie. gifts to clients, cost of holiday greetings

Home Improvements, Sales and Refinances

Investment Purchases and Sales Information

The Basis of Inherited Property

Specific Uses of Loan Proceeds

Medical Expenses

Charitable Contributions — receipts for donated items

Interest and Taxes Paid

Records on IRA Contributions

Mileage

Records to Keep

Cancelled Checks - 7 years

Bank Statements - 7 years

Tax Returns - 7 years

Employment Returns - 7 years

Expense Reports - 7 years

Entertainment Records - 7 years

Financial Statements - permanent

Contracts - permanent

Corporate Stock Records - permanent

Employee Records - permanent

To replace lost or missing documents

Medicare Hotline   (800) 633-4227
website: www.medicare.gov
- To obtain or replace Medicare card - change of address
- Claims inquiries
- Information about Medical programs, Medigap insurance
- General questions and coverage information

Social Security Administration   (800) 772-1213
website: www.socialsecurity.gov
- To obtain or replace Social Security card
- Personal statement of earnings - estimate of future earnings
- Proof of current payment

Internal Revenue Service   (800) 829-1040
website: www.irs.gov
- Federal tax questions
- Form request line
- Business tax questions

The Living Bank   (800) 528-2971
website: www.livingbank.org
- Information on organ donation

VA Regional Office   (800) 827-1000
website: www.va.gov
- Obtain military documents

Passport Services   (877) 487-2778
www.travel.state.gov

TO REQUEST BIRTH CERTIFICATE

Contact the state vital statistics or vital records offices of the state where the birth occurred. Please include the following information:

Name as it would appear on birth certificate

Place of birth (City, County, State)

Hospital

Date of Birth

Sex

Race

Fees vary from state to state. Vital statistics or vital records offices also maintain records of death, marriage, and divorce. You may also check website www.vitalrec.com for further information.